D1708941

Hot Air Balloons

Dana Meachen Rau

Marshall Cavendish
Benchmark
New York

For Allison, my colorful morning riser
—D.M.R.

With thanks to Becky Wigeland, Curator, National Balloon Museum, Indianola, Iowa,
for the careful review of this manuscript

Other Marshall Cavendish Offices:
Marshall Cavendish International (Asia) Private Limited, 1 New Industrial Road, Singapore 536196 • Marshall Cavendish International (Thailand) Co Ltd. 253 Asoke, 12th Flr, Sukhumvit 21 Road, Klongtoey Nua, Wattana, Bangkok 10110, Thailand • Marshall Cavendish (Malaysia) Sdn Bhd, Times Subang, Lot 46, Subang Hi-Tech Industrial Park, Batu Tiga, 40000 Shah Alam, Selangor Darul Ehsan, Malaysia

Marshall Cavendish is a trademark of Times Publishing Limited.

All websites were available and accurate when this book was sent to press.

Editor: Christina Gardeski
Publisher: Michelle Bisson
Art Director: Anahid Hamparian
Series Designer: Virginia Pope

Printed in Malaysia (T)
1 3 5 6 4 2

Library of Congress Cataloging-in-Publication Data
Rau, Dana Meachen, 1971–
Hot air balloons / by Dana Meachen Rau.
p. cm. — (Bookworms chapter books. Surprising science)
Summary: "Discusses the basic scientific principles and historical context of hot air balloons"
—Provided by publisher.
Includes bibliographical references and index.
ISBN 978-0-7614-4873-0
1. Hot air balloons—Juvenile literature. I. Title.
TL638.R38 2011
629.133'22--dc22
2009053758

Photo research by Connie Gardner

Cover photo by Gunnar Kullenbera/SuperStock

The photographs in this book are used by permission and through the courtesy of: *SuperStock*: pp. 4(L), 8(L), 14(L), 18(L) Gunnar Kullenbera. *The Image Works*: p. 5 M. Greenlar; p. 10 Mary Evans Picture Library; p. 15 Sean Cayton; p. 12 Photo 12. *PhotoEdit*: p. 3 Myrlee Ferguson; pp. 7, 20(B), 21 Jeff Greenberg. *Corbis*: p. 4(R) Carl Purcell; p. 9 Blue Lantern Studios; p. 11 Bettmann; p. 16(T) Luke MacGregor. *Getty Images*: p. 6 Matt Cardy; pp. 8, 10(R) Hulton Archive; p. 13 Popperfoto; p. 14 Wire Images; p. 16(B) Jason Todd; p. 18(R) Richard Price. *Alamy*: p. 20(T) David Ridley. *AP Photo*: p. 17 Ben Hillyer.

Hot Air Balloons

CHAPTER 1

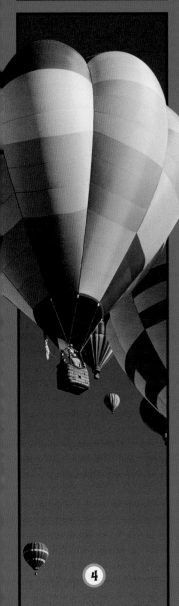

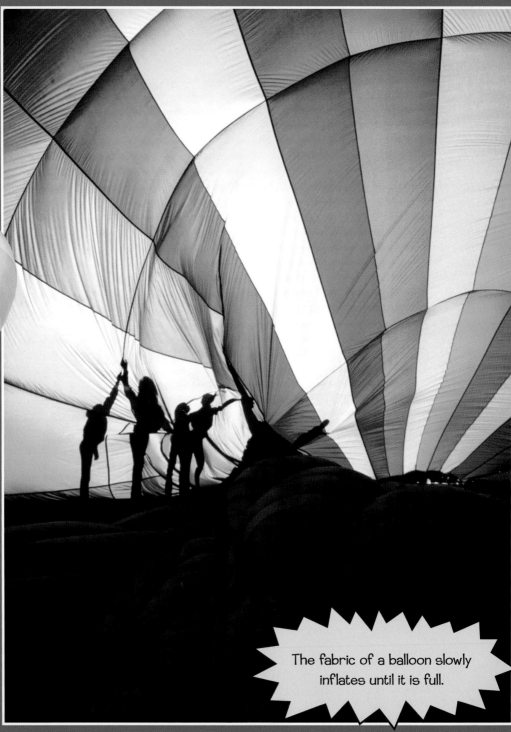

The fabric of a balloon slowly inflates until it is full.

Ready for Take Off

It is early morning. People unload a huge colorful bag in an open field. They turn on a strong fan. They aim it into the opening of the bag. The bag starts to grow. It's a balloon! But it isn't the kind of balloon you get at a birthday party. This balloon is taller than sixteen men!

Ropes hold down a balloon so it doesn't float up to the sky too soon.

Hot air is lighter than cool air. A burner heats the air in a balloon so it will rise from the ground.

Suddenly, fire roars into the balloon. It starts to rise. People climb into the basket under the balloon while others hold it steady. Then the balloon takes off, carrying its **passengers** into the sky. They float higher than the houses, higher than the trees, up to where the birds fly.

Can you imagine what it would be like to float so high? Cars would look like tiny dots. You'd be able to see for miles. The wind would be your guide. What would it feel like to ride with the wind?

Balloon riders get a bird's-eye view.

CHAPTER 2

Jean-Pierre Blanchard crossed the English Channel from England to France in a balloon.

Ballooning History

Greek stories tell of Daedalus and his son Icarus, who made their own flying wings.

Throughout history, people have wondered what it would be like to fly. The Chinese watched their kites move with the wind. The Greeks told stories of men who made wings to help them fly. People drew pictures of flying machines. But flying seemed **impossible**.

In the late 1700s in France, the Montgolfier [mont-GOL-fee-ay] brothers noticed something about paper and fire. If paper got too close to the flames, it burned. But they saw that if the paper was above the fire, the hot smoke seemed to make it float and rise. So in 1783 they made a balloon out of paper and silk. They lit a fire under it. People

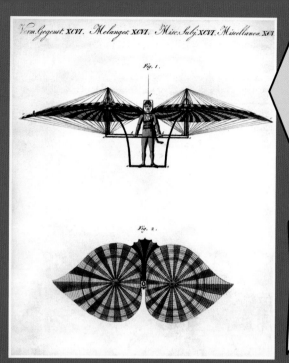

Early inventors drew pictures of unbelievable flying machines.

The two men who rode the Montgolfier balloon waved to the crowd below.

were amazed when the Montgolfier brothers sent a sheep, a duck, and a rooster as passengers in this first hot air balloon. The animals had a successful flight. Soon after, two men rode in a Montgolfier balloon. They traveled more than 5 miles for 25 minutes.

Other French people made balloons filled with a **gas** called hydrogen. Hydrogen can rise like hot air does. In 1785

Jean-Pierre Blanchard flew a gas balloon over the English Channel, a waterway between England and France. He also flew the first balloon in America. George Washington watched Blanchard's balloon **launch** in 1793 from Pennsylvania on its way to New Jersey.

Ballooning became very popular. Pilots tried flying balloons higher and farther than ever before. People found uses for balloons during war. Balloons could carry messages. They could spy from the sky.

Soldiers used balloons to scout out the battlefield.

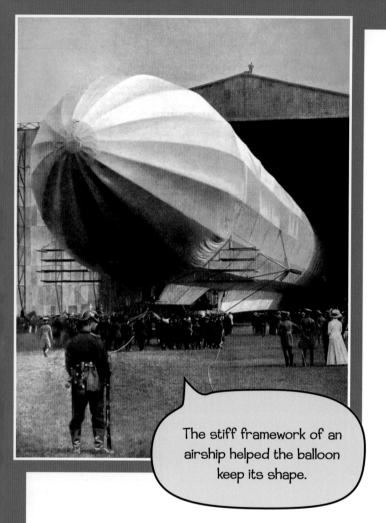

The stiff framework of an airship helped the balloon keep its shape.

By the early 1900s, **airships** flew in the sky. An airship had a gas-filled balloon with a frame to give it a sausage shape. The basket in which people rode, called the gondola, was enclosed and often very large. It also had an **engine** and **propellers**. Pilots could steer these new types of balloons in the direction they wished to go. Some airships were used in war. Others were used for travel and the gondolas looked like fancy hotels inside.

In the early 1900s, the Wright brothers also flew the first airplane. After that, people rode airplanes for travel instead.

The Wright brothers' first airplane gave people another way to travel the sky.

But people didn't forget about balloons. They built gas balloons that could study the weather and even travel around the world. In 1960, modern hot air balloons were developed by Ed Yost, and were later used for sport. Today, people join hot air balloon clubs. Teams hold balloon races. Passengers take rides in the sky to see the beautiful land below.

CHAPTER 3

The burner heats the air inside the envelope to inflate the balloon.

How Hot Air Balloons Work

The science called **physics** helps us understand how hot air balloons rise in the sky. Physics is the science of how things move.

Air is all around you. You can't see it. But you can feel it when the wind blows. Air also has **weight**. Hot air is light. Cold air is heavy. That means that hot air rises up in the sky. Cold air sits closer to the ground.

A hot air balloon works because the hot air trapped inside the balloon is lighter than the cold air outside

Crowds wait for the big launch.

15

the balloon. So the balloon rises up into the sky!

The big balloon is called an **envelope**. Most envelopes are larger on the top and narrower on the bottom. They come in all colors. The envelope is made out of strong, light cloth called **nylon**.

Just like a paper envelope holds a letter, the balloon envelope holds the hot air. Pilots heat the air in the balloon with a **burner**. The burner sends out a huge flame into the envelope. When the balloon is full of hot air, it starts lifting off the ground.

At a balloon festival many balloons take off at the same time and fill the sky with color. Below, the parachute valve in the top of a balloon lets out hot air.

A basket hangs below the burner. This basket carries the pilot and the passengers. The basket is light, but strong enough to carry several people. Some baskets can carry up to twenty passengers at a time if the balloon is big enough to lift them.

A basket hangs below the balloon to hold passengers.

When the pilot wants the balloon to go up, he fires up the burner. This can be very loud. The flame grows bigger. It heats the air in the envelope so the balloon will rise.

When the pilot wants the balloon to go down, he pulls a cord that lets out some of the hot air. The cord opens the **parachute valve**. The parachute valve is a cut-out circle of nylon in the top of the balloon. The balloon stops rising. As more hot air escapes, the balloon sinks toward the ground.

CHAPTER 4

Balloon pilots use wind currents to push them in the direction they want to go.

Up to the Wind

You turn your handlebars to steer your bike. But a pilot can't steer a balloon. He can make it fly higher or lower, but he can't make it go from side to side. He needs some help from the wind.

Wind moves in different directions. Wind might be moving one way high in the sky. It might be moving another way lower in the sky. These paths of wind are called **currents**. A pilot uses these currents to move the balloon from place to place. He moves the balloon up and down with the burner and parachute valve. When he finds a current going in the direction he wants to go, he lets the balloon ride the wind right or left.

Pilots can't control how fast or how slow the balloon moves. That's controlled by the wind. But too much wind can be dangerous. It can tear the balloon or send it in the wrong direction.

19

So pilots always check the weather. A day with clear skies and not too much wind is best for ballooning. They often launch right after the sun comes up when the wind is calm and the air is cool. They can also launch in the evening, but must land before the sun sets.

Balloons don't usually land in the same place they started. A pilot talks to his crew on the ground with a radio. They look for a safe place to set the balloon

After the balloon lands, the crew lets out the air.

The crew folds up the balloon so it's ready for its next trip.

Check Out Receipt

Keller Public Library Pick-up Window
817-743-4800
www.cityofkeller.com/Library

Tuesday, August 20, 2019 11:22:42 AM
40741

Item: 31751002499730
Title: Hot air balloons
Call no.: j629.133 RAU
Due: 09/10/2019

Item: 31751002641224
Title: Finding Winnie : the true story of th
e world's most famous bear
Call no.: jEASY MAT 2016 Caldecott
Due: 09/10/2019

Total items: 2

Thank You!

Ride the skies in a balloon!

down. The crew meets the balloon when it lands. They will let the air out of the balloon and pack it up again.

Riding a hot air balloon is an adventure. Where will the wind take you?

Glossary

airship [AIR-ship] an aircraft that is lighter than air with an engine that can be steered

burner [BUR-ner] the part of a hot air balloon that creates a flame to heat the air inside

currents [KUR-uhnts] the flowing pathway of wind or water

engine [EN-juhn] a machine that turns energy into a force to make something run

envelope [EN-vuh-lohp] the part of a hot air balloon that holds the hot air

gas [GAS] a form of matter that floats in the air

impossible [im-POS-uh-buhl] not able to happen

launch [LAWNCH] to send up into the air

nylon [NAHY-lon] a strong, light type of cloth

parachute valve [PAR-uh-shoot VALV] a cut-out circle of nylon in the top of the balloon envelope that lets out hot air

passengers [PAS-uhn-jers] people who travel in some sort of vehicle

physics [FIZ-iks] the study of how objects move

propellers [PRUH-pel-ers] blades that spin around a center point to help a vehicle move

weight [WEYT] the measure of how heavy or light something is

Books to Discover

Hicks, Kelli. *Action Sports: Hot Air Ballooning*. Vero Beach, FL: Rourke Publishing, 2009.

Platt, Richard. *Experience: Flight*. New York: DK Children, 2006.

Priceman, Marjorie. *Hot Air: The (Mostly) True Story of the First Hot-Air Balloon Ride*. New York: Atheneum Books for Young Readers, 2005.

Rinard, Judith E. *The Story of Flight: Smithsonian National Air and Space Museum*. Toronto, Ontario: Firefly Books, 2002.

Van Leeuwen, Jean. *The Amazing Air Balloon*. New York: Fogelman Books, 2003.

Websites to Explore

Century of Flight www.century-of-flight.net

E-Balloon.org www.eballoon.org

NASA: History of Flight
www.ueet.nasa.gov/StudentSite/historyofflight.html

National Balloon Museum www.nationalballoonmuseum.com/

Smithsonian: National Air and Space Museum www.nasm.si.edu/

Index

About the Author

Dana Meachen Rau is the author of more than 250 books for children. She has written about many nonfiction topics from her home office in Burlington, Connecticut. Mrs. Rau looks forward to the day she can ride a hot air balloon to get a bird's-eye view of the world.

With thanks to the Reading Consultants:

Nanci R. Vargus, Ed.D., is an assistant professor of elementary education at the University of Indianapolis.

Beth Walker Gambro is an adjunct professor at the University of Saint Francis in Joliet, Illinois.